D1320131

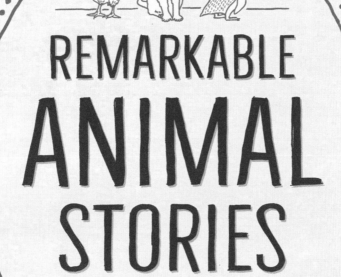

REMARKABLE ANIMAL STORIES

from New Zealand *and* Australia

Written by
Maria Gill

Illustrated by
Emma Huia Lovegrove

SCHOLASTIC
AUCKLAND SYDNEY NEW YORK LONDON TORONTO
MEXICO CITY NEW DELHI HONG KONG

For all the dedicated keepers, carers, vets, aquarists, volunteers at zoos, wildlife hospitals, sanctuaries and rescue centres — M.G.

· ·

To Dad, who nurtured
my love of painting — E.H.L.

First published in 2021 by Scholastic New Zealand Limited
Private Bag 94407, Botany, Auckland 2163, New Zealand

Scholastic Australia Pty Limited
PO Box 579, Gosford, NSW 2250, Australia

Text © Maria Gill, 2021
Illustrations © Emma Huia Lovegrove, 2021

The moral rights of the author and illustrator have been asserted.

ISBN 978-1-77543-645-4

12 11 10 9 8 7 6 5 4 3 2 1   1 2 3 4 5 6 7 8 9 / 2

Illustrations created in in watercolour and gouache

Publishing team: Lynette Evans, Penny Scown and Abby Haverkamp
Designer: Vida & Luke Kelly Design
Typeset in Adobe Garamond Pro, Belfort Draw Dark and Quimbly
Printed in China by RR Donnelley

Scholastic New Zealand's policy is to use papers that are renewable and made efficiently from wood grown in responsibly managed forests, so as to minimise its environmental footprint.

CONTENTS

INTRODUCTION

Animals can make us laugh, cry or feel loved. We care for animals because they give us so much back.

It's been recognised that animals have personalities and feelings, much like humans. Researchers studied more than 60 different species, and found that all animals show individual differences in traits. Some are shy, some more aggressive and some more trusting. Research has shown that insects can be curious, some fish are playful, reptiles sometimes like to cuddle each other, and birds can experience terror and pride. Mammals are thought to feel all of the above as well as love, loyalty, joy, grief and shame. It is because of these shared emotions that we're drawn to them.

When I interviewed wildlife carers, handlers or aquarists for the book, they all had stories to tell about the animals that had touched their hearts. Some animals have characteristics that make them stand out from the rest.

From New Zealand there are stories about a lovesick gannet, a talkative kōkako, a fostering takahē, a kea who tricks tourists, a grumpy tuatara, and a dolphin who gives gifts to his favourite people. There's a social-media-savvy cat, a rat catcher that's scared of sea lions, a penguin that thinks wildlife hospitals are a holiday venue, and a kākāpō that's the nation's conservation representative.

In Australia, fairy penguins surf the tide onto land together, wombats help nurse other wombats, koalas learn to trust a young koala whisperer, and we meet a kangaroo that prefers the rescue centre to being in the wild. There's also a TV-star chicken, a cheeky echidna, a famous cat, a koala-rescuing dog and some quirky, lesser-known Australian animals.

These are true stories, but they've been told in a creative and lively way so that readers can learn about the animals themselves. The animals have not been anthropomorphised (made to act or think like humans); their behaviour is exactly what that type of animal would do in the wild.

Enjoy the stories! Some might make you feel sad, but most will make you laugh. New Zealand and Australia are very lucky to have such unique creatures, and it is thanks to the wildlife centres, sanctuaries and zoos that we still do.

Maria Gill

KAHURANGI,
THE TALKING KŌKAKO

The kōkako is the last species of the wattlebird family to survive on the mainland. Each bird has its own signature call and birds in different areas have their own accent. Its large body and long, strong legs make them poor flyers. But they can hop like a kangaroo, jump from branch to branch like a monkey, and glide like a squirrel.

A ranger in the Hunua Ranges watches four kōkako chicks squirm inside their nest. They're bald, cold and sightless. But after eating lots of mushed up berries delivered by their mum and dad, they develop into plump young chicks. Their striking denim blue feathers sprout, and their beady black eyes are quick to learn from their parents. Soon, three of the young kōkako fledge and fly off, leaving only the littlest kōkako. Its chest and wing muscles are not strong enough to fly yet. The ranger worries predators might attack the wee chick, so he takes it to Hamilton Zoo.

Nicknamed Kahurangi, the Māori word for blue, the tiny kōkako thrives. It doesn't have to compete for food at the zoo, and there's plenty of it. She loves her keepers. They chat to Kahurangi and tell her she is a beautiful kōkako. After a while, she repeats the word 'kōkako'. At first the keepers think they are imagining that they hear her say it. But soon they realise they have an exceptional bird in their midst.

Sometimes, when the keepers are in Kahurangi's cage, a message comes through the walkie-talkie. To their astonishment, they soon hear Kahurangi mimicking the low growling noise of their radio. And that's not all. Spectators often wolf whistle to the parrot near the kōkako's cage. When Kahurangi wolf whistles back, the keepers can't believe it. But they worry she might have imprinted too much onto humans. They send her to Pūkaha National Wildlife Centre in Masterton so she can have more 'kōkako time.'

The new keepers release her into an aviary with several male kōkako. But Kahurangi is not interested and rebuffs the boys. She goes off her food and is grumpy. She is probably missing human visitors – they entertain her.

The keepers recapture Kahurangi and place her in her own cage where she thrives once more. When they clean her pond, she thinks they're having a bath and joins in. She often gives gifts to her favourite keepers. It might be a special little leaf or a twig she is proud of, clutched in her claw.

YOU'RE A BEAUTIFUL GIRL!

I KNOW!

One of the keepers notices that visitors often talk to Kahurangi, so the keeper teaches her some new words. Now when people say, "You're a beautiful girl," Kahurangi answers with, "I know."

One day, a German film crew asks if they can video Kahurangi after unsuccessfully filming wild kōkako. Kahurangi appears to be delighted when they set up in her cage. She sits on their heads and flicks her wings. Then she peers into their viewfinder to see what they're looking at. The keeper places her in front of the recorder, and she immediately flies back on top of the camera. They get some good close-ups, but not much else!

Kahurangi hasn't forgotten all her bird behaviour, though. Every year she lays several infertile eggs. But if a crowd gathers around her cage, she leaves the eggs and goes to chat with the spectators. The eggs grow cold.

Kahurangi is everyone's darling. Some people visit regularly just to see her. She has touched many hearts.

HENRY, THE OLDEST TUATARA IN CAPTIVITY

When an almost-70-year-old tuatara arrives at the Southland Museum in 1970, he's nicknamed Henry, after King Henry the Eighth, who had six wives. Reptile keeper Lindsay Hazley figures the tuatara may have just as many partners over his long lifetime. But Henry's a slow starter.

Lindsay releases Henry into an enclosure with his first wife, Stephanie, whose partner has just died. Henry climbs the highest rock, raises his head and stretches out his long tail to show her how much mana he has. However, she's grown used to having the place to herself and is not keen to share it with a high-and-mighty male. She chases him all around the enclosure. Lindsay builds a wall between them.

Many years later, when Lindsay releases the pair into an outdoor enclosure, Henry reclaims the space as his and adopts the role of boss. After the ground freezes one winter, Stephanie goes off her food. Lindsay brings her inside, but she doesn't recover.

That year Lindsay finds another wife for Henry. But Henry ignores Mildred. Lindsay wonders if he needs competition to arouse his interest. Soon Albert and Lucy arrive. Henry can see his rival in the neighbouring enclosure. They're very busy making babies.

Frustrated, Henry decides to put a stop to their activities.

Male tuatara have a crest of spines that they fan out to attract females. They shed their skin once a year and can live for 60–100 years.

One Friday evening, Henry digs a hole, kicking the soil towards the window. Then, when the dirt is piled high, he climbs up and over the wall into Albert's enclosure. Henry chases Albert round and round the pen for three days. If Lindsay hadn't interfered, Henry would have fought Albert to the death. It takes Albert a year to recover from his injuries.

Back in his own enclosure, Henry grows more and more grumpy, biting Mildred's tail. He's put in solitary confinement. One day, Lindsay notices that a lump that's been on Henry's backside for a while has turned nasty. The vet takes a sample. Lindsay is shocked when he receives the news that it is cancerous. No wonder Henry is bad-tempered! The vet removes the lump, and Lindsay lets Henry recover after the operation for a while before he releases him back with Mildred. This time, instead of trying to bite her, he draws himself up to his most regal bearing and, in broad daylight – unheard of in tuatara behaviour – mates with Mildred. In 2009, Henry becomes a dad for the first time at 111 years old! It makes headlines in 270 newspapers around the world.

When an Australian zoo asks if they can have a male tuatara, Lindsay chooses frisky Albert and moves him into an enclosure on his own to prepare him for his trip. Every day, he can see Henry sunbathing with Lucy and Mildred. Albert is distraught. And then they delay his departure, prolonging his anguish. So much so, according to his keeper, he dies, heartbroken.

Meanwhile, Henry is very content with his two wives. Every couple of weeks, Lindsay feeds the threesome home-grown locusts, mealworms, and Henry's favourite – juicy huhu grubs. Like a flock of hens, they scrabble towards the food and swallow it whole. They'll even climb up Lindsay's knee to snatch whatever insect he is dangling from his hand.

The threesome will stay at the Southland Museum tuatarium, while all their babies are flown to the Marlborough Sounds and released onto a predator-free island. Tuatara are returning to their homeland under the guardianship of the Ngāti Koata iwi. But the chief ambassadors for tuatara, Henry and his wives, still have important work to do – they're showing the public the last remaining line of an ancient order of reptiles that lived alongside the dinosaurs.

FLINT, A RODENT DETECTION DOG

If a Department of Conservation (DOC) dog trainer hadn't seen the little dog when he did at the pound, it most likely would have been put down. But the trainer thinks the Jack Russell–fox terrier cross could be useful. He names him Flint, and he soon becomes a highly trained rat detector. But he has a flaw that could cost him his life.

Flint loves scent training with Richard Johnston, his dog handler. He soon learns to find rats and mice from their poo, pee, nests and trails on what should be pest-free islands and mainland sanctuaries. If Flint picks up a scent, Richard marks it on his GPS and gets out of the area quickly. He doesn't want the rodent to pick up their scent and scarper. Instead, a trapper will come in to catch the pest.

On one assignment, Richard takes Flint on board the Royal New Zealand navy ship *Canterbury*. After he's checked the ship is rodent-free, Flint settles into the cargo hold for the journey to Campbell Island, a subantarctic island far to the south of New Zealand. Flint is soon a favourite with the naval crew. They're amused at this tiny dog with the big attitude. He lets them pat him while he's off duty, but as soon as Richard puts on his jacket and muzzle, he's working and ignores all humans except Richard.

Once on the island, the pair make sure all the gear brought over with them is rodent-free before relaxing in the base hut. Richard calls Flint to come with him to look around. But the dog refuses to leave. Richard peeks his head out of the hut and sees that a sea lion has just waddled past. Flint cowers in the doorway. Richard laughs. "You'll have to get used to the wildlife around here, boy, there's plenty of it."

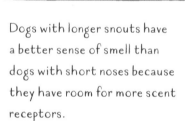

Dogs with longer snouts have a better sense of smell than dogs with short noses because they have room for more scent receptors.

Over the next week and a half, they search coastlines, harbours, gullies, streams and ridgelines to see if they can pick up any scents. Richard aims for the smelliest hotspots – a rotting carcass, rockhopper penguins sitting on their nests, and sea lion colonies – that's where rats and mice are likely to hang out.

On their last day, Flint's little legs struggle to climb through the cutty grass and swamps. He jumps over mounds and runs through streams. It's exhausting work. Every now and then Flint cowers behind Richard … and a sea lion pops out of the shrubbery.

When they arrive at a massive seal colony, Flint doesn't know where to hide. The bull seals aren't used to humans – or dogs – and roar their displeasure at the intrusion. Elephant seals charge at them from every angle! When two bulls rush towards Richard, Flint bolts. Richard holds his ground with the two noisy males and they back off. Then he calls Flint, and spends hours searching for him. Richard worries Flint's jacket might have snagged on a bush, or that he might be barking in response but the wind is swallowing the sound, or he's run so far he can't hear Richard calling.

It's getting dark and the navy ship radios that they're sending a helicopter to pick them up. Distraught, Richard watches the thermal camera imaging on their way back to the ship, hoping they'll pick up some sign of Flint. But they see nothing.

Richard phones everyone who he thinks might be able to help, but it takes a while to put a plan into action. Everyone is quiet on board, missing the plucky little dog.

Two days later, Heli Otago volunteers to try and rescue Flint. They radio to say they'll be arriving at the base hut in fifteen minutes. Richard hopes Flint is there. If not, they'll need to search the island and it'll be like looking for a needle in a haystack. An impossible job. He's tense all afternoon, knowing that if they don't find him, Flint – wearing his working muzzle – will starve to death. Then, over the intercom, he hears that they found Flint sitting on the base hut veranda – sure that someone would come back for him. A cheer echoes over the boat and everyone's in a festive mood. The little dog with the big attitude is coming back!

BARNEY & PEBBLES,
THE CARING WOMBATS

When Brigitte Stevens lays eyes on Barney the wombat, it's love at first sight. But he needs help. The humid weather in Queensland is making him sick. Brigitte packs up her home in Brisbane and moves to South Australia to set up a southern hairy-nosed wombat sanctuary with Barney at her side.

Barney teaches Brigitte wombat body language, how wombats like to be treated, and how to live harmoniously with nature. It is a steep learning curve at first, but soon Brigitte's sanctuary is brimming with orphaned wombats. Sixteen years later, in 2020, the sanctuary is home to 86 young wombats, who are free to wander around the property and choose to live either in burrows or in any of the three houses on the property. Brigitte, with Barney's help, places bedding around the houses, in the back yard and even in the burrows for the little wombats to snuggle up in when they go to sleep.

At mealtimes, Brigitte grates 18 kilograms of carrots for the toothless young wombats. She warms up rice milk for the babies and the odd older spoilt wombat like Pebbles, who demands a warm drink each night before bed.

Pebbles came to the sanctuary in 2018, after being stolen from her mother. Barney welcomed six-month-old Pebbles and helped her settle into her new home. When Barney died of old age later that year, Pebbles took over his role, becoming Brigitte's helper and greeting the other wombats on her rounds.

Pebbles is not as disciplined as Barney was though. Pebbles bounces around Brigitte's feet, turning in circles, giving herself a fright when she bumps into other wombats or trees. Then she stands still, wondering if anyone has noticed her clumsiness. She also chats in wombat language in a loud voice, waking up the sleepy wombats.

If Brigitte sits down or crouches to pat a wombat, Pebbles runs up and climbs onto Brigitte's lap. She presses her nose against Brigitte's lips, wanting a kiss. When volunteers come to help plant native plants, Pebbles is right there with them, getting in everyone's way. But they can't resist her cuddles and kisses.

On very hot days, Pebbles naps near other wombats in their long burrows, where it's cool. Wombats love to dig and are always renovating their burrows. Brigitte discovered one of the burrows was 6 metres deep and 50 metres long. Wombats don't mind sharing their burrows with other animals, including snakes – not an arrangement that is particularly favourable to the wombats!

When it gets even hotter, Pebbles comes inside the house, where the air conditioning is turned on 24 hours a day. She and numerous other wombats have taken over Brigitte's house. Every bed and couch has wombats curled up asleep during the day.

The wombats can wander off into the wild when they're older if they want but there's not much food to find and the territorial wild wombats tend to chase them until they're exhausted. Wombats are friendly and trusting animals and are quick to imprint on humans, which is another reason why they tend to stay in the sanctuary. Here they'll get their daily feed of horse pellets, carrots and warm milk – an arrangement that suits Brigitte, Pebbles and the other wombats just fine.

Wombats are the world's largest burrowing animal, and the smartest marsupial.

They excrete cube-shaped poo, which stops it from rolling away when they mark their territory.

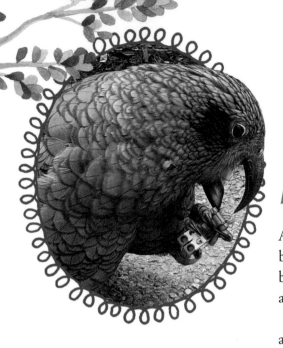

KEN-JOE,
A CHEEKY KEA

A ranger tags four-month-old Ken-Joe the kea with pink and white bands just after he fledges. Even though he has learnt how to find berries, leaves and insects in the wild, Ken-Joe starts hanging out with a gang of kea, who soon teach him it's easier to steal from tourists.

Ken-Joe struts around the tents camped nearby, chewing on poles and cords. If a tent is unzipped, he will go inside and rummage through backpacks for anything he can eat. He likes a bit of bling too, stealing shiny objects and decorating neighbouring tree branches. One of his favourite antics is to pinch undies and socks and drape them over leaves so everyone can see them!

Ken-Joe often strolls into the Arthur's Pass store, much to the dismay of the owner. The mischievous kea grabs anything in reach and races out with the store-owner shooing him from behind with a broom. The kea isn't scared though and tries it on most days.

Sometimes he partners up with his sister Joan. While one of them entertains a tourist having their photograph taken, the other sneaks behind them and steals sandwiches out of their bag.

Ken-Joe occasionally swings up onto the top of a caravan or campervan as it is being driven off and takes a joy ride. He clutches onto the rail, enjoying the wind ruffling his feathers, then flies off to his next escapade before they get up too much speed.

He might fly to one of the huts and stamp on the roof. Then he slides down the roof and hangs upside down from the window to peer in. It looks to the people inside as if he is laughing at their surprised faces.

For a while Ken-Joe appears to be off his game. He is so dozy he lets a ranger catch him and take him to the South Island Wildlife Hospital. The vet takes a blood sample to see if Ken-Joe has lead poisoning from his days of chewing on various car parts. The test results show his lead levels are very high. The vet injects Ken-Joe with medicine into his chest muscle twice a day for five days.

Every afternoon, carers coerce him into a smaller cage and place him in a windowless room. When he comes back to his cage it's clean and food has magically appeared. The carers don't want kea to get used to being fed by humans, so always put him in another room so he can't see who is filling up his food boxes. Ken-Joe spends hours figuring out how to prise apple slices and other fruit out of pinecones, cardboard tubes, toys and boxes. It keeps him busy and takes his mind off trying to escape.

After the first round of treatment, the vet tests him again and, finding his levels still too high in lead, subjects him to five more days of injections. Ken-Joe urinates frequently, but that means the medicine is doing its job. He is peeing out all the poisonous lead in his body. Finally, the vet gives Ken-Joe the all-clear. He is well again.

The ranger releases Ken-Joe back into the wild in June 2019 … but it doesn't take long before he is spotted getting back to his trickster ways.

Unlike most birds, kea have a large forebrain, which enables them to problem-solve, communicate, and even have a sense of humour. Some say they are the world's most intelligent bird—and are even more clever than dolphins!

PADDLES,
THE PRIME MOGGIE

Member of Parliament Jacinda Ardern and her partner, Clarke Gayford, visit the SPCA to find a pet. As soon as they spy a ginger cat with six 'toes,' including 'thumbs' on each paw, they fall in love. They call her Paddles, take her home and she keeps them entertained. Little do they know that Jacinda and Paddles will soon become famous.

When Jacinda becomes Prime Minister of New Zealand, she accepts congratulatory calls from Prime Ministers and Presidents from around the world at her home in Point Chevalier, Auckland. While on the phone to the US president, Paddles pushes through the cat flap, jumps onto the chair next to Jacinda and meows hungrily for food. Clarke hastily grabs the cat and takes her out of the room.

Later that day, Jacinda introduces the public to her cat, holding Paddles in her arms while talking to the television crew outside her home. Not long after, a new Twitter account starts under the name 'Paddles, First Cat of New Zealand.' It says, 'Have thumbs, will tweet. Not affiliated with Labour Pawty. Bullies will be scratched/blocked.' Soon it has 11,400 followers. Cat and dog lovers from around the world are tweeting comments back and forth to Paddles. Even the dog belonging to the American ambassador to New Zealand sends tweets!

At first, people think Jacinda or Clarke are tweeting on behalf of Paddles, but they aren't. It still is not known today who it was; the tweeter chooses to stay anonymous.

Then disaster strikes. While Paddles is crossing the road to the Prime Minister's house, a car runs her over. A neighbour picks up the injured cat and takes it to the vet, but they can't save her. The man, who accidentally backed his car over the cat, apologises and his children write a letter asking the Right Honourable Jacinda Ardern not to send their father to jail. She sends them a card saying sorry for the grief it has caused them.

Meanwhile, cat lovers around the world mourn the moggy. The US Ambassador's dog, Gracie, tweets: 'My Mom, Dad and I are very sorry to hear about @FirstCatofNZ. We will say a prayer tonight.'

One person suggests that surely Paddles should have a state funeral.

PM Jacinda Ardern tweets: 'Thanks for everyone's thoughts. And on behalf of Paddles, please be kind to the SPCA. They found her before we did, and we will always be grateful for that."

Clarke Gayford recommends that gifts of condolence be made to the SPCA in memory of their crazy little 'sleep anywhere' ginger cat. The SPCA is very grateful for the donations sent on behalf of Paddles.

For a while the mysterious tweeter keeps the cat's Twitter page going, but changes the name to 'The Ghost of Paddles'.

Cats with more than four toes on their paws are called 'polydactyl'. It's a genetic abnormality that can affect any breed of cat, though it's rare for a cat to have it on all four paws.

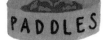

PADDLES

CRIKEY & PUMPKIN, KOALA HOSPITAL CHARACTERS

On a remote rainforest island near Queensland's Great Barrier Reef, the Bee family have set up a koala hospital. The frightened baby koalas that are brought to the centre might have been abandoned by their mother, or she could have been attacked by dogs or run over. Older koalas are rescued because they're ill, or green ants have attacked them and they're now blind. And with the big drought in 2019-20, the quality of the eucalyptus leaves is poor, and many koalas are starving.

Vet Ali Bee, husband Tim and their 12-year-old daughter Izzy get up at first light to feed the baby koalas in their lounge. After breakfast, Ali takes the youngest koalas with her to work at a vet clinic on the mainland, because she needs to feed them twice during the day.

When Izzy gets home from school, she helps clean the six koala enclosures: kindergarten and nursery enclosures for the babies, primary and junior school enclosures for those learning to climb trees, and female and male adult enclosures. Izzy also helps her dad cut fresh eucalyptus leaves and branches from a neighbouring plantation.

When Ali gets home, Izzy helps her mum treat the koalas with ointments for those who need it. Izzy wants to be a vet when she grows up, and she learns from watching her mother. Ali says Izzy is like a koala whisperer.

ointment

The babies are frightened and traumatised when they come in. But not for long. Izzy cuddles the tiny babies and encourages them to drink their milk. She never forces them. They learn to trust the girl and before long they're sucking on the bottle. Izzy is always the first to get them eating leaves, too. She crushes a leaf and lets them smell it, then pulls off bits to put in their mouth. Some of the babies need a leaf milkshake to get used to the taste. Some even need a poo smoothie! Mothers usually feed babies their poo and it helps them build good bacteria in their gut.

Every koala has its distinct personality and they are all cute, but two have stood out for Ali and Izzy. Crikey feared anyone coming near him when he arrived. Like other koala babies who have lost their mother, he had given up. Izzy said she wanted to look after him and spent every spare moment cuddling him and encouraging him to eat. If she hadn't, he would have died. From then on, they had a special bond and he only had eyes for Izzy. After a year it was time to release Crikey back into the wild. Izzy was sad letting him go, but knew it was for the best.

Pumpkin is their other favourite koala. She's one of the smallest they've had at the clinic and the most active. "She's a bit like a spider monkey," says Ali. Pumpkin jumps around the enclosure, hanging on all fours from the top, and then leaps down and scurries around the cage. She lets the boys in her cage know she's the boss, too.

The Bee family will care for plenty more characters over the years and every single one of them will leave an imprint on their hearts.

Often called 'koala bears' because they resemble teddy bears, koalas are more closely related to wombats than bears!

INKY,
THE GREAT ESCAPE ARTIST

A fisherman hauls a crayfish pot onto his boat to see if he has caught anything. An octopus the size of a rugby ball stares back at him. The scarred cephalopod holds onto the trap lid with its shortened limbs. "Looks like you've had a rough time," the fisherman says.

Later that day he drops the octopus off at the Napier National Aquarium where he knows they'll take good care of it. A keeper fills a tank with water and transfers the octopus into it. He makes sure the lid is on securely, knowing it might try to escape. Then he watches the mollusc settle into its new home.

The aquarium staff hold a competition to name the octopus and a hundred children respond. The winner suggests 'Inky' because octopuses squirt ink when they escape from predators, allowing them to hide unseen.

Inky becomes a popular attraction at the aquarium, and visitors are fascinated to see the keeper drop jars of food into Inky's tank. Inky snatches one and unscrews the lid, then thrusts its tentacles in to pull out the mashed-up fish. Sometimes the staff hides food in toys, and Inky has to problem-solve how to get it out. Like other octopuses, it has an intelligent brain and excellent eyesight. Before long, its tentacles find a way inside the toy to prise out the seafood.

Over four months, Inky's body fills out and looks much healthier. Whenever the keeper visits, Inky comes out from under its rock to say hello. When he puts food or objects into its enclosure, Inky touches his hands. Sometimes Inky sticks its suction pads onto the edge of the glass to watch what he is doing.

The keeper finds out Inky is female when she lays lots of little eggs. She would have mated before she came to the aquarium, but stored the sperm until she judged it a safe time to fertilise her eggs. Tragically, however, the eggs disappear. The staff believe they may have been sucked out through the tank's filtration system.

Octopuses only live two years, and once they breed, their job is done. Inky dies a natural death soon after.

A month later, another octopus arrives at the aquarium and staff give it the same name. The keeper doesn't know if it is a male or female because all octopuses share the same body type, but calls it 'he'. Inky II is an adventurous octopus who constantly explores his tank.

Considered the most intelligent of all invertebrates, octopuses are the animal kingdom's greatest escape-artists. They have no bones in their body and that enables them to squeeze through the tiniest of cracks. But mostly they'll hide in plain sight, changing colour and pattern to blend in with their surroundings.

One day, the keeper is in a hurry and doesn't put Inky's lid back on properly. Inky waits until the middle of the night when the aquarium is deserted. He uses his suction pads to climb up the glass tank, forces his body through the tiny hole left open, and slides down the side of the tank. Inky then crosses the floor of the aquarium, leaving a wet trail behind him. When Inky finds a drainpipe, he squeezes himself through a 150mm-wide funnel, and slithers out into the open sea.

The keeper figures Inky would have crept fast along the sea floor until he found a rocky reef. For the next few weeks or months, he might have explored a reef environment and maybe even chased some female octopuses until he found a mate. Meanwhile, back at the aquarium, Inky's escape has made newspaper headlines around the world. Two children's picture books are even written about Inky's escape to freedom. He has been immortalised in print!

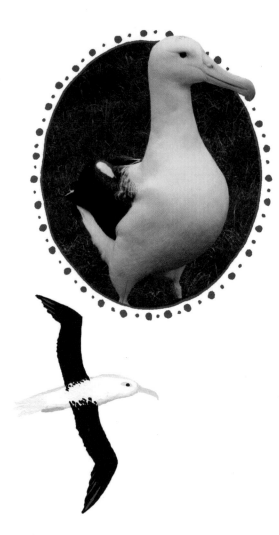

ROB, AN UNLUCKY-IN-LOVE ALBATROSS

The ranger at Taiaroa Head on the South Island of New Zealand clips Red, Orange and Blue bands around the young albatross and nicknames him R-O-B. Several weeks later, the fledging jumps off the cliff, flies north then heads east towards South America. For several years, he spends his days soaring the skies, and fishing and bobbing on the Pacific Ocean, his webbed feet never touching land.

At five years old, Rob yearns for a partner. And he knows the best place to find one. He flies south then west, back to the place where he hatched. Rob waddles around the Taiaroa headland checking out all the females. He stretches his 3-metre long wings and calls, "Yak, yak, yak!" But no one takes any notice.

Throughout the spring months, everyone pairs up, except Rob. He waddles around the reserve to make sure he hasn't missed anyone. He hasn't. He will have to try again next season.

The next year, Rob is first to return to Taiaroa Head. And after exercising his exhausting courtship dance for several weeks, he's successful in finding a mate. They cuddle and twirl their necks around each other and hang out with the other 'teenagers,' socialising late into the night.

The next year the pair meet back at the Reserve and Rob builds his mate a nest. She settles on the grass clippings and ruffles her feathers. And they wait. Other pairs lay their eggs, watch their hatchlings sprout and feed them through the hot summer months. Rob and his girl aren't so lucky.

On their third unsuccessful attempt, the rangers take pity on them and give them a fertile egg from another nest. The doting parents fuss over the hatchling and help it grow into a plump chick. They bid it farewell at the end of the season. Rob can't wait to raise another one.

The next year, he prepares a nest for his loved one and settles. Albatrosses land to his left, right, in front and behind … but not his partner. He waddles around to see if he's missed her. He hasn't. Rob gives up his vigil after several months and takes off for his migration early.

Albatrosses have flat eyes that enable them to see above and below the water. They have ridges above their eyes that act like sunshades, protecting them from the sun.

Six years pass before he finds another partner, GOY (Green, Orange, Yellow). Goy and Rob happily raise a chick together. Rob is the most attentive dad on the headland. He flies out to sea, swallows a fish, and then regurgitates it into the chick's mouth on his return. It grows into a fluffy albatross.

Sadly, his partner doesn't return on their fourth anniversary. Nor does his next partner, after one year of courtship. The rangers don't know whether sharks have killed the vanishing females, or if perhaps they've consumed too much plastic and starved to death, or been caught on a fishing line.

Over the next ten years, Rob is often the first back and the most energetic courtship dancer. But no girls are interested. At the end of the season, he stomps to the cliff edge and flies off. A little forlorn, but determined not to give up. The rangers feel sorry for Rob and can't understand why he is so unlucky in love. He looks the same as the other albatrosses.

They wonder if his song or courtship dance is a bit clumsy for the discerning girls.

They needn't have worried. Just when Rob thinks he'll never find a mate again, he does. He performs his dance many times before she notices him, but finally, a female albatross beckons him. Rob waddles towards her, and they sing together. At last! He can't wait to build her a nest.

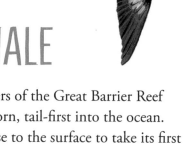

MIGALOO,
THE WHITE WHALE

Early one August, in the warm waters of the Great Barrier Reef lagoon, a humpback whale calf is born, tail-first into the ocean. Its mother uses her fins to help it rise to the surface to take its first breath of air. The other females gather around the newborn. It is white! They haven't seen an albino before.

When the calf is strong enough, the pod of females and their young swim southwards to Hervey Bay in Queensland. The shallow waters are warm and safe and nosy males aren't likely to interfere. The white calf feeds from its mother's rich milk and grows strong. It must, it's got a long trip ahead.

In early October, the pod migrates down the coast of Queensland and New South Wales, out past Tasmania and all the way down to Antarctica. The white calf's mother eats krill, herring and mackerel twice a day to build up her reserves. Her calf relies on her milk until it's 11 months old.

Throughout the Antarctic summer months, the humpback whales feast and the calves grow bigger. The albino copies its mother, opening its mouth wide and letting the fringed overlapping plates

Humpback whales can sing for up to 22 hours at a time! You can hear a great recording of whale song on YouTube called 'Humpback Whale song from Monterey Bay'.

hanging from each side of its upper jaw (called baleen plates) filter out the water and capture the schools of fish and krill.

At the end of the season, it's time for the pod to swim back, passing through the Cook Strait in between the North and South Islands of New Zealand, then straight to Cape Byron in Australia. They fast while migrating, then dine on small fish when they reach the tropical waters along the New South Wales and Queensland coast. At the end of the Australian winter, the young white whale travels with the pod back to Antarctica.

Humans sight the albino for the first time in 1991, in Byron Bay, when it's around three years old. An Aboriginal tribe on the Sunshine Coast call the whale Migaloo, meaning 'White Fella'. Researchers take photographs of its unique serrated tail flute. They notice it has a raised bump just below its dorsal fin and two further down, and this helps identify it.

The researchers take a skin sample and identify Migaloo as a male. That is confirmed when he starts singing at around 15 years old. He's letting females know he would make a great partner. His unique haunting song is long and carries far. Humans cannot hear his high-frequency sounds in the quiet spaces.

Over the next two decades, sightings of Migaloo are frequent. It helps the researchers track the Eastern Australian humpback group's migration from Australia to Antarctica and back. Sometimes Migaloo returns from Antarctica looking yellow. Worried onlookers think he is unwell and notice that he's a lot skinnier than when they last saw him. The yellow coating is an algae that he's picked up in the cold waters. And he's thinner because he doesn't eat when he's migrating. But researchers have also noticed that his skin looks red around his blowhole and think he might be getting sunburnt. This could lead to sun cancer in his later years.

To protect Migaloo, in 2013 the Queensland and Commonwealth Government pass a law saying they would fine any vessels that come within 500m of any white whale. They are determined to try and protect Migaloo and others of his kind.

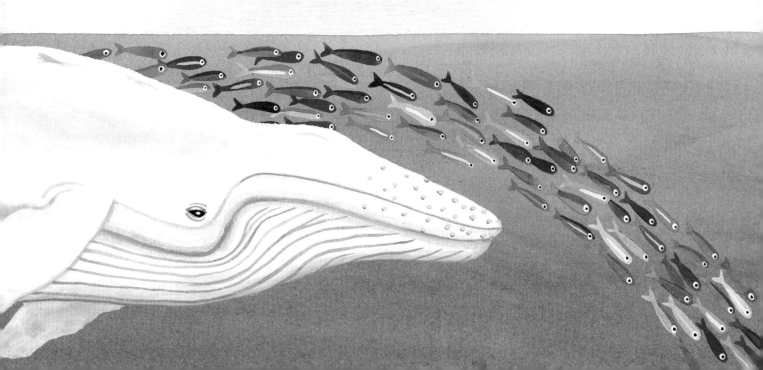

NIGEL NO-MATES, THE LONELY GANNET

On windswept Mana Island, a ranger, with the help of volunteers, installs twenty concrete gannets on the side of a cliff. They also arrange solar-powered speakers to boom out the gannet call, beckoning the seabirds to nest. Then they wait, hoping gannets will return to this predator-free island, where once they nested.

Eighteen years later, a solitary gannet lands on the clifftop. It waddles around the concrete gannets, checking them out. One stone-faced gannet attracts him. The male gannet bows and then fences with her stony bill. He hopes his courtship dance tells her he would like her as a partner.

A visiting scientist nicknames the lovesick gannet 'Nigel' and watches him chat to his loved one. Nigel curls his neck around her and tries to groom the gannet. Tap, tap, tap, his bill clinks on her stony body.

Even though the concrete bird does not respond, Nigel flies back every day after foraging off the western shores of Wellington. He lands with a thud and waddles over to his girl. Nigel winds his long neck around her graceful throat in a loving embrace. Then he raises his bill skyward as if to tell her he'll return soon. After flying around the island, the gannet plucks seaweed from the shallows and brings it back, drooping like a lei from his bill. He drapes it over the hard earth, stomps on it, and then squirts his guano all over it. From under trees he gathers twigs, places them on top of the mound, and then squirts it some more. He lets it harden under the hot sun.

Hungry after his nest-building exertion, he jumps off the cliff and glides out to sea, searching for shadows under the water from 30 metres above the waves. When he spots a school of piper fish, he dives, torpedo-like, reaching a speed of 145 kilometres per hour before plunging into the sea. He grabs a small fish in his serrated-edge bill. Back on the surface he swallows it whole, lets it digest, and then flies back to the clifftop to nestle next to his loved one.

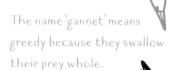

The name 'gannet' means greedy because they swallow their prey whole.

One year later, another male gannet flies in. It is given the nickname Norman. Nigel does not like this intruder in his territory. He advances on Norman, forcing him to step away from his nest and partner. Norman isn't fooled by the concrete birds though, and soon flies off, hoping to find a real bird.

But Nigel is not one to give up. He stands by his mate, season after season.

On a balmy January evening in 2018, after three years of hoping his mate might return his love, Nigel dies next to the concrete decoy. The ranger finds his lifeless body and breaks the news to the Friends of Mana Island (FOMI) volunteer group. One of them writes a post about it on social media. It strikes a chord with animal lovers around the world and goes viral. Everyone is saddened that Nigel most likely died broken-hearted.

Meanwhile, the FOMI group and the ranger have cleared the vegetation around the decoys and repainted them, hoping more gannets will nest there soon.

PHAR LAP,
THE BIG-HEARTED HORSE

The big, ungainly chestnut colt has long legs that often trip him up in his first year. The owner sees nothing special in him and sells him at New Zealand's Trentham horse sales. Australian trainer Harry Telford takes a punt on the horse he's never set eyes on, convincing one of his owners to buy him solely based on his pedigree. When the horse arrives in Australia, the man who put up the money is not happy. The 15-month-old horse is a big gangly thing, with a face covered in warts and an awkward gait. Harry offers to train him for free and nicknames him Bobby, although he registers his racing name as Phar Lap, derived from a Chinese/Thai word for 'lightning' – a name he will soon live up to.

Six months into his extensive training, groomer Tommy Woodcock bustles Phar Lap into a horse trailer and in February 1929, takes him to his first race. The starting gun fires and the horses burst out of the starting gate. The noise and proximity to strange horses frightens Phar Lap as he gallops around the track. He finishes last. Phar Lap loses his next three races too. Harry isn't worried though; he knows the two-year-old must develop the will to win. When Phar Lap wins his 5th race that season, Harry knows his instincts about the horse are right. In the second season that year, Phar Lap is entered for another 10 races. He wins four and places twice, including a third at the 1929 Melbourne Cup.

In the first season of 1930 (February to May), Phar Lap wins nine out of ten races. In the AJC Plate, he dominates from start to

finish, smashing the Australasian record for the 3.6-kilometre race. The Australian Prime Minister Bob Hawke says it is "the single most remarkable performance in Australian turf history."

Phar Lap does even better the next season (August to November), winning 10 races. But organised crime gangs try to stop him from entering the Melbourne Cup, the premier racing event of the year. They send Harry threatening letters. Harry ignores them, thinking they're a hoax, until Tommy rings him in distress. Someone had just tried to run him and Phar Lap over! Harry confides he's received another letter saying they'll shoot him next time. And they try! But fortunately they miss. Harry organises for Phar Lap and Tommy to go into hiding, taking no chances. On race day, they arrive at the track late and under a police escort. Phar Lap gets his revenge, winning the 1930 Melbourne Cup lengths ahead of the other horses.

The following February, Phar Lap astounds the crowd once again at the 1931 Futurity Stakes. Left behind at the start and splattered in mud from the horses' hooves in front, Phar Lap is trapped behind a wall of horses. The jockey drops him back to last, then takes him wide of the field. In the final approach to the finishing line, Phar Lap accelerates and slowly gains on the leaders, winning by a neck! He continues to win all but two of his races that year.

But winning all these races has drawbacks. To make it fairer, horses who keep winning are made to carry extra weight. Phar Lap is handicapped with the heaviest weight ever put on a horse his age. So the owners decide to race him in America, where he won't have a handicap. After a long voyage on a ship and a 15-hour journey in a horse float, he arrives in Mexico in sweltering heat. Phar Lap has never run on a dirt track before and one of his hooves has split. And though he's famous in the Southern Hemisphere, he's a nobody in America. But Phar Lap shocks the racegoers by beating the horse favoured to win by two whole lengths. Afterwards, he's named one of the world's top ten racehorses of all time.

After his sudden death in 1932, Phar Lap's heart was found to be more than 1.5 times as big as a normal thoroughbred's heart.

CHRYSTALL, A PENGUIN SHARK ATTACK SURVIVOR

While swimming off the coast of the Catlins, a little yellow-eyed penguin, who has only recently left her mother's care, suddenly finds herself in trouble. A big barracouta fish attacks her legs! Then a shark smells the blood and lunges at her belly, leaving a large gash. By the time the little penguin washes up on Chrystall's Beach, her infected wounds need immediate veterinary care, or she'll die.

Lucky for the injured penguin, a conservation officer finds her and takes her to the Dunedin Wildlife Hospital. The nurses name her 'Chrystall' after the beach where they found her.

Dr Lisa Argilla examines Chrystall and cleans her wounds. The injured penguin doesn't struggle even though she is frightened. It's as if she knows the woman is trying to help her. A nurse pours electrolyte water down a tube in Chrystall's throat to rehydrate her, along with pain relief and antibiotics to treat the infection. Then they leave Chrystall to recover from her ordeal, hoping they have saved her in time.

Two days later, the vet x-rays her and takes blood samples. Over several days they operate on Chrystall four times. After the anaesthetic, she wobbles around her pen like a drunken sailor until the drugs wear off! The nurse tucks Chrystall in a crate for her trip to Penguin Place.

The Penguin Place carers feed Chrystall lots of fish, fattening her up before she moults. When penguins lose their feathers during moulting, they cannot swim to hunt food, and must rely on their fat reserves to see them through the fast. The carers also insert a micro-chip in Chrystall's neck before they release her, so they can track her. With the entire yellow-eyed penguin population down to just 700 birds, every single one is precious.

The next time one of the penguin keepers sees Chrystall, she is sitting on a nest, incubating an egg. They are thrilled she has recovered enough to become a mum.

Not long after, while trying to build up her reserves before the next moult, Chrystall is attacked by a shark. Finding herself brought back to the Wildlife Hospital, she swaggers confidently out of her transport crate and makes a beeline for the enclosure she was last in. She knows the routine.

Every morning, she body slams the hospital door to let the vet and the nurses know she wants to explore the ward. Chrystall supervises the nurses while they make breakfast for the other injured animals. If she feels they need to work faster, she gives them a nip on the back of their legs. While they dish out the food, Chrystall walks behind them, greeting the other patients.

When it comes time to release Chrystall, the Penguin Place carers are sure she won't be unlucky enough to get attacked again … or will she?

One year later, she's back at the Wildlife Hospital with another shark bite to her belly. She struts out of her transport crate and races to her usual pen then skids to a stop. There's another animal in her place! Disgruntled, Chrystall nips the nurses to show she's not pleased.

When Penguin Place carers film her release months later, she scurries towards a pair of yellow-eyed penguins to greet them. They squawk, and the male attacks her. It's not the reaction she expected.

The carers hope that next time they catch sight of her, she'll be sitting on a nest, not needing hospital and rehab time again. Flippers crossed!

Yellow-eyed penguins are one of the rarest penguins in the world. Their Māori name, *hoiho*, means noise shouter. The yellow around their head and in their eyes is the same chemical found in carrots!

LITTLE MISS SUNSHINE, THE TV STAR HEN

A little brown hen balances on poop-crusted wire bars in her sloping cage that's so small she can't even flap her wings. She surveys the thousands of birds squawking as they lay their eggs – it's deafening. She chokes on the strong ammonia smell and notices something unusual.

Men and women from Edgar's Mission Farm Sanctuary are opening cages and taking bewildered hens outside. Is this the end? The little hen squawks when it is her turn. But instead of holding her upside down, the person carries her in the crook of their arm, pats her neck and talks in a soothing voice. She is placed gently into the back of a car. Not used to standing on a flat surface, she falls over, then flaps her wings and perches for the first time, on top of a car seat. Soon after, the motor starts, and they drive away. Over the course of that week, 1080 chickens are rescued from the battery hen farm.

At the sanctuary, the hens are released inside a large barn, smelling of fresh hay. They are thrown grain and the hens scratch at the floor and peck, their natural instinct showing them how to be a normal hen.

The next day, the doors slide open and the little brown hen wanders outside into the sun. She struts like a stilted goose, her legs unused to walking. In the middle of the penned area, the hen scratches the earth, lies down and billows dust up and over her body. A young child watching the hen delight in her first dust bath says to her Aunt Paula, "We should call her Little Miss Sunshine." Paula agrees that is a fine name. She goes back to training a chicken called Marilyn Monroe, who is a bit of a diva. Paula notices Little Miss Sunshine watching through the glass door.

One day she decides to teach Little Miss Sunshine some tricks too and she soon becomes her star pupil.

Paula shows Little Miss Sunshine how to ring a bell. Each time she tolls it, Paula clicks a clicker and gives the hen some grain. Soon Little Miss Sunshine can identify a chicken badge from other animal badges and can even find it when partially hidden. Scientists thought only humans had this skill.

Paula teaches Little Miss Sunshine many more tricks and is surprised how quickly she learns them. She can count, come when called, and follow directions. Paula takes Little Miss Sunshine to schools, businesses and field days to demonstrate how clever chickens are.

On a school visit, Little Miss Sunshine amuses the young audience when she jumps off the stage and runs off. Paula hears the hen squawking and finds her inside the pigeonhole where children put their school bags. She is happy to perform her routine once she has laid her egg!

Little Miss Sunshine and Paula feature in a TV commercial called 'Ain't a way to treat a lady' with the message that we should treat farm animals with kindness and respect, not make them lay hundreds of eggs in horrible cages. Their message makes its mark, as more chicken farmers realise what they're doing is cruel and ask the team to take their birds too.

Meanwhile, Little Miss Sunshine moves into Paula's house, wearing a nappy so she doesn't poop inside. She eats her meals with Paula and hangs out with two rescue dogs. She's enjoying her much-deserved freedom.

The record for the most egg yolks in one egg is nine yolks! Most eggs are laid in the morning between 7 a.m. and 11 a.m.

GUS,
THE DOG-CAT

When Glenn Druery's best animal mate, Bob, dies of cancer, Glenn decides to replace him with a cat. Glenn lives most of the time on a yacht and feels it isn't fair to keep a dog on deck. "But the proviso is that the cat comes on our adventures with us, just like Bob did," Glenn tells his partner Melissa. Soon after, Gus, a three-month-old Tonkinese cat joins them.

On Gus's first day on board, Glenn drops his kayak into the sea, slips in and then taps the side. Gus leaps towards the kayak but misjudges the distance, flies over and lands in the water. Most cats would be terrified. Not Gus. He paddles back towards the dock. Glenn plucks him out of the water and lifts him onto his shoulders, where he sits throughout their paddle. Afterwards, Glenn hoses the seawater off Gus, who seems to think it is all part of the procedure. From then on, Glenn and Gus kayak most days. On one trip, Gus spies a seagull ahead. He crawls down from Glenn's shoulders and creeps to the front of the boat. When they're one metre away, Gus launches into the water. The seagull squawks and flies off. Gus turns around and paddles back. Some days, Glenn drapes Gus over his shoulders and jogs down to the local dog park. On the way back, Gus runs through the shallow water alongside Glenn. On other days, Glenn takes Gus cycling or swimming. Gus takes it all in his stride, watching the world from his best mate's shoulders.

Gus also accompanies Glenn to his Government office job every day, as well as visiting Glenn's mother each week at her rest home. On one visit, a 90-year-old man is sitting weeping, missing his family and not adjusting to rest home life. But as soon as he sees Gus, he springs out of his chair and asks if he can pat the cat, forgetting he's upset.

Just before Christmas, Glenn enters Gus in the Scotland Island dog swimming race. His dog Bob had won it five years earlier, and Glenn decides what's good for Bob is good for Gus. In the training sessions, the two swim every day to build up their stamina. When Gus is tired, Glenn swims underneath him and Gus climbs onto Glenn's shoulders. One day, Glenn deviates from his usual breaststroke and

Tonkinese are a Siamese/Burmese cross-breed. Burmese have a dog-like temperament: energetic, people-oriented and they enjoy a swim. Looks like Gus has inherited this!

turns over onto his back. Gus climbs to the highest ground – which happens to be Glenn's face – and sits down.

On the day of the big race, hundreds turn out to see Gus compete alongside the 70 dogs. Glenn stands 20 metres away from the other competitors. Then, when the horn blows, he rushes into the water with Gus on his shoulders. Melissa paddles nearby in the kayak. Gus swims alongside, then crawls back onto Glenn's shoulders when he's tired. When a dog comes within a metre, Glenn whisks Gus onto the kayak. The dog doesn't even turn his head, too busy concentrating on the race. Gus wins first prize in the cat category (in which he's the sole competitor). The crowd chants, "Gus! Gus! Gus!"

TV, newspaper and radio media hijack Glenn and interview him on the spot.

After Gus's TV and radio appearances he's world famous – even clinching roles in two upcoming films. Glenn makes sure the fame doesn't go to Gus's head by ensuring life is kept as normal as possible – cycling, kayaking, running and swimming every day of the week. Gus nips Glenn's heels if life gets too boring.

BIG MAMA,
THE ENIGMATIC ECHIDNA

Big Mama, a short-tailed echidna, saunters towards a bull ant mound. Big Mama stirs up the dirt with her back feet and then steps back. The biting ants swarm to where she's been digging, ready to attack. Meantime, Big Mama sneaks round to the back of the mound and slurps up their eggs. Her diversion has worked; she's had a feed and not been bitten.

Further on, Big Mama sees some birds foraging in the leaf litter. The echidna butts the birds out of the way and takes over their patch, swirling her 16-centimetre-long tongue to catch the insects. The indignant birds fluff up their feathers and squawk in protest, but Big Mama is not leaving until she's had her fill.

As she waddles around, the back spurs on her feet emit a smell that attracts male echidna. Soon she has a train of nine males following her. Twenty-two days after a male echidna mates with Big Mama, she curls into a ball and lays one jellybean sized-egg into her pseudo-pouch.

Days later, a bald puggle struggles out of the leathery egg. When the puggle is 50 days old it no longer fits in its mother's pouch, and hangs underneath. If it were to fall off, Big Mama wouldn't be able to pull it back up. It would be at the mercy of bull ants and other predators.

Instead, Big Mama digs a burrow and leaves the young echidna inside. Every five days she checks in and feeds the toddler milk, then two hours later she'll wander off. For 160 days, the young echidna's spikes grow. One day a goanna pokes its head into the burrow. The scared puggle rolls itself into a ball. The goanna sniffs it but decides the spikes are too sharp.

Echidna were around when dinosaurs roamed the earth.

Even though it's a mammal, an echidna lays eggs like a reptile.

It leaves, hunting for less prickly prey.

When the echidna is 7 months old, its
mother stops feeding it milk. The young echidna
will stay in the burrow until it is 12-18 months old,
then it leaves, never to return again.

When a fire rages on Pelican Lagoon, Big Mama burrows
into the ground, covering her body and spikes with dirt. She slows
down her body temperature and metabolism and goes into a deep
sleep called 'torpor'. She stays there for several weeks, not emerging
until the fire has stopped and the ground has cooled. She rises out
of the ashes like the prehistoric creature she is, snorting dust out of
her nostrils. Everything is charred. But that's not a problem for Big
Mama; her kind have survived many fires, an ice age, and droughts.
She claws open burnt logs and finds termites, then digs deep for
insects that have hidden in the dirt.

To cool herself down, Big Mama swims in the lagoon, paddling
her stumpy legs. In the cooler dusk hours, she strolls across a log and
does a back flip and rolls over. She's not frightened – she's playing.
She runs to the other end, scrambles across the log like she's walking
on a tightrope then backflips and rolls again.

When Big Mama sees one of the resident scientists – Dr Peggy
Rismiller – she freezes, hoping Peggy won't see her. Peggy picks up
Big Mama, checks her transmitter, then releases her. Big Mama
scurries away, into the Kangaroo Island bush haven; she's a survivor
and will be around for many years to come.

CALVIN, A GREEN TURTLE SURVIVOR

A newly hatched green turtle struggles out of its broken shell buried in the sand. It feels an urgency to scrabble along the beach and into the warm tropical sea as quickly as possible, and joins a throng of baby turtles heading in the same direction. Just as it enters the frothing tide, a gull swoops down to pluck the hatchling from the sea. The terrified baby turtle dives below the surface in the nick of time and paddles with dogged determination out into the ocean.

When it is five years old, the turtle yearns to travel further and swims into the East Australian current, relaxing in the warm water flow. While napping, it inadvertently drifts into cooler waters.

The green turtle swims closer to the New Zealand land mass. It nibbles on sea grasses and sips the water, but the water is foul and makes the turtle sick. It uses all its waning energy to escape a shark. A boat skids over its shell and the turtle has only enough strength to paddle onto a remote Northland beach, exhausted.

Later that day, gentle hands lift the weary turtle from the sand and drive it to Auckland Zoo. The Conservation Medicine Centre vet checks the green turtle all over. He takes some blood tests and x-rays the reptile. Then he injects the turtle with antibiotics and medicine and forces electrolyte water down its throat to help it rehydrate. It is fed cut up fish and then left to sleep and recover.

One week later, the green turtle is sent to Kelly Tarlton's Marine Centre. There, aquarist Maddy Seaman checks it over and sees it is still in terrible condition. She hopes the sickly turtle (now named Calvin) survives. Maddy follows the vet's instructions, giving the turtle medicines and water in his trickle bath.

The green turtle's shell is olive to black in colour, but they have green fat beneath their shell, probably because of the sea grasses they eat.

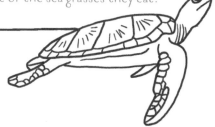

Soon, Calvin stops resisting the hand-fed fish and looks forward to his daily feeds. He knows it is lunchtime when Maddy taps a stick with a red dot on the black tank. His appetite has come back, and the turtle greedily eats the food. Afterwards, he stays perfectly still while Maddy scratches his back. She can tell he likes it and scratches some more.

Three months later, Calvin has gained five kilograms in weight and is ready to go into the big tank with all the other marine animals. But the colourful fish frighten him! There are so many of them, in all shapes and sizes. Two pigfish headbutt him and steal his food. But Maddy is onto them. She throws chopped fish in the opposite direction to distract the greedy fish while she hand feeds Calvin.

Calvin feels drowsy afterwards. He rubs his back against a rock for a while, then drifts lower down and hides under an upturned boat, away from the noisy fish, bright lights, and curious tourists. He snoozes most of the afternoon until he hears Maddy tapping against the tank. Feeding time again.

Early in March 2020, Maddy and the other aquarists who have been looking after Calvin place him into a crate and drive from Auckland to the far north of New Zealand. After his long journey, he spends the night resting in a motel shower to stay wet and cool. The next day, at Rangiputa Beach, two local school children carry him down to the water's edge with a crowd looking on. Calvin's flippers flap when he sees the sea. The children sing a song before releasing him into the water. He shoots off like a rocket ship, excited to be back in his natural environment. Calvin might hang around for a while in the sheltered waters of Rangaunu Harbour, before catching a ride on the warm water currents back to the tropics, ready to find a partner. Maddy and the aquarist team wish him luck!

LITTLE BLUES, THE SURFING PENGUINS

It's mid-summer and the sun is going down; it's time for the fairy penguins to return to their nest. A group of penguins form a raft and ride the surf onto the beach. From above they look like one enormous animal and it scares off predators thinking of attacking.

The penguins with prime real estate find their nests on the sand. The rest waddle through the dam, across the dunes, over the scrub, and climb up the hill to their burrows. They share their regurgitated fish with their babies.

One penguin climbs up and over a fence put there to keep the penguins out. The penguin waddles towards his burrow, alongside the new visitor centre. It takes a while for the wildlife officers to find how he is getting in each night. They position cameras all around the fences and then one night they see him. The wildlife officers build him a nesting box, on the right side of the fence, to replace the burrow they've pinched off him.

When it's dark, the last of the penguins come ashore. Chicks whose parents haven't returned beg and accost each penguin who pass them. They're hungry and are convinced someone will give in to their pleas. Most don't.

After the chicks have been fed and they've quietened down, the parents go outside their burrows to socialise with their neighbours. They sing and chat, staying up late partying. There are no humans to disturb them – the government bought all the houses and shops on the peninsula, removed all the buildings and declared it a sanctuary.

The penguin population, which had dropped down to 10,000 birds, recovered to 32,000 once the land was returned to the penguins. It's the highest population of blue penguins in the world.

Before dawn, many of the penguins return to the sea. Some will stay out for 4-6 weeks. The penguins are happiest in the water, spending most of their time there. When the little blue penguins tire, they take micro naps, sleeping minutes at a time. As soon as they're awake, they're hungry. They search for small fish, swallowing it whole. Their flippers act like wings and they fly through the water, back to their sanctuary, ready to feed their babies.

The young penguins who have recently fledged won't come back for a couple of years, though. They explore the region and when they return, they're ready to find a partner. They waddle to the burrow they hatched in and will fight with their parents over ownership. If a penguin and his partner are successful and hatch a chick, they'll stick together for many years. If not, they'll divorce each other and find someone better the next year.

If the penguins ever get caught in an oil slick, the Phillip Island team are prepared. They've been sent thousands of woollen jumpers from all around the world – penguin size.

The carers slip the knitted jumpers over the penguins' heads to prevent them spreading oil over their body when they're preening their feathers. The toxic oil makes them sick and it's impossible to get the smeared oil off them. Thankfully, there hasn't been an oil spill for a while. But the conservationists are still being sent thousands of jumpers. Now the penguin plush toys in the visitor centre wear them. It helps raise money for the endangered penguins, ensuring their sanctuary is a safe place for them to thrive.

Little blue penguins are the smallest penguins in the world at around 25cm tall and weighing 1kg.

ROYAL, THE REGAL KIWI

Kiwi keepers Averill Moser-Rust and Bethany Brett are on the West Coast looking for an egg from a specific kiwi in the Paparoa Ranges. Once found, they bring it back to Willowbank Wildlife Reserve, clean it and check it for any damage. Then it is placed into an incubator.

When the egg is around 80 days old, a Great Spotted kiwi (Roroa) chick heaves with its feet and cracks open the narrow egg. But its hips are stuck and no amount of struggling helps it budge. After 48 hours, the keepers slightly widen the crack in the shell and the chick wriggles out. With a tummy full of yolk, the young kiwi tries to stand using its pink bill to balance, like a three-legged stool.

Averill weighs the chick (a female), checks her all over, and then puts her back into the incubator. Averill writes the chick's new name on her notes – Royal. It's an in-joke between Averill and Beth, as their nicknames are Queen and Princess.

Each day Beth reduces the temperature inside the incubator until it eventually resembles room temperature. Royal is now ready to go into her own brooder box. When the girls clean it, Royal runs around and tells them in kiwi language that she's not happy with the intrusion. Once the chick has pooped out all the egg yolk she absorbed while in the womb, she's ravenous. Averill and Beth feed her daily with a kiwi powerpack meal of minced ox beef, vegetables and fruit, wheat germ and vitamins. Once Royal regains her birthweight of 300 grams, Averill and Beth put her in one of the outdoor enclosures. Each day she snoozes in a man-made burrow. During the night she probes the soil hungrily for insects; she's got a big appetite for such a small kiwi.

Near Royal's enclosure, Lala is attacking Averill and Beth's gumboots, which they've hung up inside the enclosure, ready to put on when they visit her. They check Lala's weight and overall health and let her go. She races back to the unattended rubbery boots and attacks them with new vigour.

Also close by is Piki. He tends to chase the keepers when they're in HIS enclosure. He weaves between their legs, trying to trip them up.

But Royal isn't interested in making friends with neighbouring kiwi. These endangered ratites prefer their own company, except when they are looking for a partner and have some offspring. Then she will take

Conservationists realised if they cared for kiwi until they became teenagers and reached 700 – 1000 grams, they could increase the birds' chance of survival considerably. While they're in an egg and a small chick, predators (ferrets, stoats, weasels, dogs and cats) could kill them. But over that weight, kiwi can out-run and defend themselves from all but the dogs.

on the important job of laying eggs. Royal and her male partner will look after the chick for the first three weeks of its life. But first, she must gain weight.

When she weighs 700 grams, Beth and Averill take her to Atarua Sanctuary, north of Greymouth. In this predator-free sanctuary, she can grow into an adult without fearing stoats, weasels, ferrets, feral cats, or dogs. After she reaches 1000 grams – the magical weight that enables her to outrun most predators – she's transferred to the South Paparoa Range, free to roam and, when she's about three years old, to find a partner.

Averill and Beth are happy to have watched her come full circle and become a full-grown wild kiwi at last.

WALLY, A PLAYFUL PLATYPUS

An adult platypus weaves her duck-like bill back and forth in the murky freshwater river. Her super-sensitive, rubbery bill can detect movement from other living beings and she's zeroing in on her prey. She scoops up the water bug along with gravel from the muddy bottom. When the platypus breaks the surface, she rolls over onto her back and uses the gravel stored in her cheeks as teeth (because she's toothless) to crush her food.

Then she's off again, letting the folds of skin droop over her eyes and ears, and her nostrils close with a watertight seal. She paddles her webbed feet and steers with her beaverlike tail to the riverbank, where she hauls herself onto the shore. The webbing retracts on her paws and she crawls on her toenails to a burrow already begun. Most likely the home of a rakali (water rat), but that doesn't put her off. She's running out of time.

The platypus keeps digging tunnels until she constructs a chamber-like room and seals herself inside. She lays two soft eggs and curls around them to keep them warm. Ten days later, two jellybean-sized babies use their egg tooth to hatch out of their shell. They're naked, blind and totally reliant on their mother. They instinctively suck milk from special hairs on her body. But each night she abandons them to hunt for food, leaving them vulnerable to predators.

Once they've grown fur, the four-month-old platypus pups leave their mother and make their own way in the river. The smaller pup digs out a burrow to sleep in during the hot summer months. One night, he meets a water rat at the entrance to the burrow. The rat lunges at him and they splash into the water. Round and round they roll, each trying to get on top. For a while the rat looks like he's winning. The young platypus shakes him off and dives deep, but he's injured. He drags himself ashore, breathing hard. He is too weak to return to his burrow.

A holidaymaker sees the sickly platypus and takes him to David Fleay's Wildlife Centre, just over the border on the Gold Coast. The rangers tend to his wounds and check on him every four hours. They feed him worms and other insects, but even with all that extra food the young platypus doesn't put on enough weight. They name him Wally and release him into a purpose-built platypus enclosure.

Each morning the rangers greet Wally at 8 a.m. Like a typical teenager, he prefers to sleep in. He yawns and won't get up until midmorning. The keepers don't touch Wally. They're wary of the venomous spurs on his ankles. The poison can kill animals as big as dogs.

Later, Wally takes a dip in the display tank, catching small crayfish and water insects in the water. Afterwards he climbs up the specially constructed waterfall and dives off into the tank. He'll do that several times before crawling under a palm set up on the water's edge. Or he might float atop a piece of driftwood for a while or sunbathe on a rock. When he's tired, he'll waddle through a tunnel and sleep in a little den.

For most tourists, it's the only chance they'll ever get to see this elusive animal that is unlike any other creature on Earth.

Platypus and echidna were around in the time of the dinosaurs! They are the only mammals in the world that lay eggs.

Platypuses are smaller than you may think — only about 38 centimetres long.

TUMBLES, THE FOSTERING TAKAHĒ

The ranger plucks out a spotted egg from a grassy nest in the Murchison Mountains, leaving one for the wild takahē to raise. He carries it back to Burwood Takahē Centre, the hub of the Department of Conservation's takahē recovery programme, and places the egg in an incubator. Just after it hatches, he swiftly puts it under a takahē-shaped brooder. Each day the chick is fed via a glove puppet resembling a poorly dressed takahē. At eight weeks of age, the keepers place the chick with foster parent birds.

One day, a young girl called Sophie Smith visits Burwood Centre and watches the young male tumble over its super-large feet. She tells the ranger they should call it Tumbles, and he agrees. Later that night, Sophie writes to the Mitre 10 hardware store chain and suggests they sponsor the takahē. With only 200 birds in existence in 2005, they need all the help they can get. Mitre 10 assists with building pens, and from then on, takahē foster or raise their own chicks, passing their parenting skills on to the next generation. It changes Tumbles' life, too.

At Te Anau Bird Sanctuary, the keeper partners Tumbles with a female takahē, but she's not his type. Nor is the next. He doesn't show any interest until he's released into a pen with Kawa. Tumbles turns his back on her and spreads his stubby wings, showing off their magnificence. Then he looks over his shoulder to make sure she's watching, but she never is; too busy pecking the grass. He steps it up with a little bobbing movement. He continues his mating dance for a couple of weeks, hoping he'll wear her down. Then, one day, she realises she likes that boy.

But she has competition. An elderly takahē sees Tumbles on the other side of the fence and hauls herself up over the wall, jumping into their pen. Kawa is outraged. She charges towards the old bird and pecks her. Catherine Brimecombe, the takahē carer at the centre, chases the elderly takahē out of the pen.

Scientists thought takahē were extinct until Dr Geoffrey Orbell found 250 in the South Island in 1948. Most were moved to predator-free islands around New Zealand to increase their chances of survival.

Soon Tumbles and Kawa lay two eggs. When inspected, they're found to be infertile. The keepers remove the duds and place a fertile egg under Kawa. When it hatches, the pair fuss over the little chick, but continual wet and cold weather weakens it, and it disappears. The next year, they raise another hatchling, and it also vanishes. Catherine wonders if a bird of prey might have caught them.

Then, success! Kawa and Tumbles fuss over their first hatchling, and hide her for the first two months. They're determined not to lose another chick. A local kindergarten names the chick Tawa. When she's six months old, she's taken to tussock boot camp and learns how to be a wild bird at Burwood along with other young takahē. A pair of older birds dutifully teach them how to strip the tussock of edible food. The juveniles must know these skills before being released into the Murchison Mountains – the site where conservationists found the last remaining wild takahē population after thinking they were extinct.

Ehara, their second hatchling is one of the first youngsters released at Gouland Downs on the Heaphy Track, after 100 years with no takahē sighted there. When the third chick hatches, local iwi Ngāi Tahu's kapa haka group blesses the chick at a special naming ceremony. They sing, and say a karakia for the bird, then name him Timata. And now, Timata himself is a proud first-time parent at Burwood Centre.

For their contribution to the takahē breeding programme, Tumbles and Kawa become stars, featuring on TV1 News' Goodsorts. With the help of takahē foster parents the takahē population is growing … just!

EINSTEIN, THE HUGGING CAMEL

Emma Haswell rescues two young camels at a Victorian salesyard and arranges for them to be delivered to her farm, Brightside Farm Sanctuary, in Tasmania.

At first the young camels are too scared to eat. Emma fills a bucket with food and stands back. It's a week before they feel comfortable enough to scoff the food in her presence. Very soon they become firm favourites with the visitors and volunteers who visit the farm.

Albert, the older camel, stays in his paddock behind the fences and respectfully keeps his distance around humans. He loves to cuddle his brother Einstein and chums up with Beauty, a steer who hopped into their paddock for company.

Young Einstein, however, has a mind of his own. If Emma is talking to a volunteer, Einstein huffs, steps over the fence with his long legs and stands between them. When Emma or the volunteer step back to talk around him, Einstein moves back to block their view again, indignant that he is being ignored.

Camels have three eyelids, two rows of eyelashes, and can squeeze their nostrils shut to keep out the sand.

When Einstein sees Emma patting the cat in the shed, he steps over the fence, barges into the barn and lays his head on the bench between the cat and Emma. His big brown eyes signal that Emma should pat him and not the cat. Another time, while Emma sits up on a hill taking videos for their Facebook page, Einstein gallops up the hill and knocks the phone out of her hand. He's incensed she's looking at the phone and not at him.

But when small children come to visit, he walks slowly towards them and lays his head on the ground so that they can pat him on the head. He's also fascinated with baby animals. He walks over fences to greet new baby lambs, calves or piglets. He sniffs them all over, very gently.

Then, when Emma gives a talk, with up to 60 people sitting in the barn listening, Einstein is back to his mischievous best. He squeezes in between chairs and knees to stand in the middle of the room. He likes to be the centre of attention.

When older children visit, he pinches their hats, teases them, and weaves amongst them. Sometimes he gets over-excited and his legs fly in every direction so Emma has to lead him out of the way in case he accidentally hurts someone.

Emma wishes she had trained him when he first arrived. It would have made it easier when he had to have an operation. Einstein watches the vet give Albert an injection and operate on him. But when it comes to Einstein's turn, he has a drama-queen meltdown, collapsing on the ground and groaning. They have to postpone the operation and do it later, when he has forgotten the vet's intentions.

Most of the time he's adorable. Especially when he and Albert hang their heads over the fence, humming, trying to encourage the volunteers to feed some of the pigs' food to them. Emma wishes all camels in the wild could live peaceful lives like Albert and Einstein.

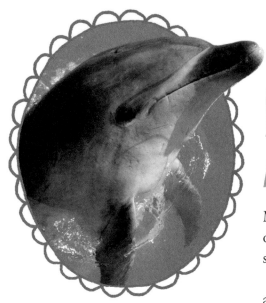

MOKO,
A VERY PLAYFUL DOLPHIN

Moko, a juvenile bottlenose dolphin, turns up at Mahia Beach, south of Gisborne, on a summer's day in 2007. He is curious about the swimmers and their toys.

When a group of children throw a ball around to each other, they aren't expecting a dolphin to join in. The trouble is, Moko doesn't want to give it back! He's like a child who won't share their new toys. The children chase after Moko, but he thinks it's part of the game. In the end the kids give up; they are no match for him. Disappointed the game has finished, Moko throws the ball up in the air and catches it, almost as if he's showing off, and then returns it to the kids.

Moko begins stealing swimmers' surfboards, then he trails them around the cove, having a joyous time. When the swimmer can't keep up, Moko brings the board closer, teasing them. But when they try to grab it, he always keeps it just out of reach. Sometimes he will pull swimmers along on a boogie board around the beach. He doesn't like it when people hang onto his fins, but he does love it when they massage him with seaweed.

Moko also enjoys playing with swimmers even when they have no toys. But sometimes Moko won't let the swimmer return to the beach because he doesn't want his playmate to go. One lady hangs onto a buoy, exhausted and cold, until someone rescues her. One day, Amy Taylor, a filmmaker shooting a documentary on Moko, floats in the

Dolphins like to chat, using a variety of sounds such as whistling, clicking, squawking, squeaking, moaning, barking, groaning and yelping.

water, not moving. Moko is concerned for her and echolocates underneath her, perhaps using his sonar to see if she is okay. When she still doesn't move, he pushes her 20 metres towards the shore.

Mostly, children and swimmers enjoy playing with Moko. Holidaymakers come from far away to see him. He has made headlines in New Zealand and overseas. Everyone wants to meet the friendly dolphin. Moko shows his appreciation, giving gifts such as sea horses to his favourite people. Once he gives a dead baby hammerhead shark to Amy Taylor and wants her to play catch with it, just like a dog with a stick.

Moko isn't just friendly with humans, either. One day a pygmy sperm whale and her calf swim through a narrow channel and become trapped between a sandbar and the beach. Conservationists try everything to rescue them. Just when they are about to give up, Moko charges towards the pygmy whales and communicates in high-pitched squeaks and squeals. He nudges their snouts, as if to say, "It'll be all right, just follow me." It seems to calm the mother whale. Moko then guides them through the channel and out to sea, checking now and then to see if they are following him.

Conservationists figure he has been separated from his pod at a young age and craves company. To protect him, and sometimes the swimmers, several minders spend the summer months in the water with Moko. One of the minders says that Moko gives unconditional love and just wants to play. Another minder, who has a special connection with Moko, has a sleepover in the water with the dolphin. She cradles him in her arms while Moko sleeps.

In 2013, Moko is voted one of the world's Top 10 Most Heroic Animals of All Time. As well as saving the pygmy whales, he taught thousands of people that dolphins are extraordinary mammals that have personalities and feelings, not unlike humans.

CHARISMA, A WINNING HORSE

When Mark Todd, a New Zealand eventing rider, first sees three-year-old Charisma, he thinks it's a shame that the horse is too small and fat. He doesn't even consider riding him in upcoming competitions. But, eight years later, when his usual eventing horse falls ill, he has no choice. Charisma has been showing promise with other riders. Perhaps Mark can get him into shape in time.

Mark brings Charisma home to his farm and nicknames him Podge. The little horse loves his food and eats everything in reach, including his bedding. Mark replaces the hay with paper clippings.

Each day, he exercises Podge on his farm, and finds him to be a sweet-natured and willing horse. Even though Mark's 1.9-metre frame towers over the 1.6-metre high (15.3 hands) gelding they seem to fit like a glove. Within months he takes him to the 1983 National One-Day and Three-Day Event Championships and wins all his competitions. It qualifies them to compete at the 1984 Olympics.

Early in February 1984, Mark flies Charisma to England. Mark worries Podge will find the enormous crowds frightening. He needn't have. Charisma strides onto the course, head held high, loving the attention. He surprises the horse community when he places second in the Badminton Horse Trials. Who is he, and who are his parents? Nobodies!

Charisma arrives in Los Angeles for the Olympics as one to watch. During the Three-Day Mixed Event, Mark and Podge are on track to win the silver. They are coming fourth in dressage, have recorded the fastest time in the cross-country, and jumped cleanly in the show-jumping. Mark hands Podge over to his groomer and rushes off to watch the gold medal contender Karen Stives jump her last round. A hush falls over the crowd while Karen and her mount, Ben Arthur, ride the course. Suddenly, everyone gasps. Ben Arthur has knocked a fence down! Mark's mouth drops open. Does that mean he just won gold? He has! The first New Zealander ever to do so in an equestrian event.

Over the next four years, Charisma wins 13 major competitions, including the British Open Championship. After a fall over a water jump at the World Championships in Australia, Podge finishes tenth.

Charisma's groomer always put a couple of small toys on the ledge of the horse's stable, wherever he performed in the world. He would throw them around his stable and try to drown them in his water bucket—just for fun!

People say Mark should retire him. But in his next Three-Day event in Germany, he wins easily. By the time Mark and Podge travel to Korea for the 1988 Seoul Olympics, they are super-fit. But critics still have doubts about Charisma being a suitable horse. He's 16 years old, considered too elderly for that level of competition. Mark thinks Podge is in excellent form and has every confidence in him.

Charisma storms out of the box like a charging bull, has the fastest time on the cross-country course, and only knocks down one fence in the show-jumping. They win Olympic gold easily in the Three-Day Individual Competition, only the second pairing ever to win back-to-back Olympic gold medals with the same mount. Charisma is now the most famous horse in the world. Mark ships him back to New Zealand and tours him around the country for six months. The fans love him. He poses for the cameras and waits patiently while they pat him. Afterwards, Mark feels Podge deserves retirement.

Back on Mark's Cambridge farm, Podge is a calming influence on all the younger horses. For 14 years, he is a special guest at many events and is a favourite with the crowds. When he dies aged 30 years old (85 in equivalent human years), newspapers around the world report his passing.

RIP Charisma!

LULU, THE CUDDLY KANGAROO

While driving home one evening, Mandy Watson is horrified to crash into a red kangaroo. She rescues the baby from the dead mother's pouch, takes it home and calls it Midnight. The joey thrives with special milk formula. Word gets out around the community that Mandy wants to help orphaned kangaroos, and soon she has 20 joeys in her crowded apartment! It's time to move. She and her husband Marc buy a 10-acre block near Kununurra and build enclosures and a shed to care for the rescued kangaroos.

Over the next sixteen years, Mandy rescues 700 kangaroos as well as numerous wallabies, sugar gliders, wallaroos, emus and wild birds at Kangaroo Haven in Western Australia. In 2020, she has 19 baby joeys in her lounge: pinkies (furless), aged 4 to 5 months, and velvets (just furred), aged 5 to 8 months. Twenty-seven older joeys hop around outside. When they no longer need milk at 18–24 months old, Mandy releases them into nearby conservation parks.

Lulu comes into Mandy's care after children rescue the baby kangaroo from her dead mother's pouch. Mandy collects the dehydrated pinky, wraps the cold baby in a warm blanket and feeds her special milk. Afterwards she massages Lulu's stomach, helping her to go to the toilet. Next, Mandy rubs Lulu's body with pawpaw cream to stop the silky skin from drying out. Then she lays the drowsy pinky in a cotton pouch to sleep.

Mandy continues the routine of feeding Lulu every four hours, along with the other babies in her care. She takes Lulu along with the other pinkies and velvets to school with her every day, where she works as a teacher aide. During the breaks she bottle-feeds the babies with the help of some of the children. And after school, Mandy feeds them again.

For the first five days, Mandy keeps a close eye on Lulu, knowing that some babies often give up, too stressed to keep on living. Luckily Lulu is one of the plucky ones. One month later, she grows fur and joins the velvets. At nine months old, she graduates to the big kids' enclosure outside, playing with the older joeys and hopping in and out of her pouch. Whenever Mandy comes into the enclosure, Lulu jumps on Mandy's lap for a cuddle. When Mandy wears her fluffy dressing gown, Lulu tries to jump headfirst into the pockets.

After 18 months at Kangaroo Haven, Lulu is ready to go back into the wild. Mandy and Marc drive seven hours to Barrbem Conservation Park and release her with a mob of joeys. They stay for a while to check the joeys are settled, and then drive off. Mandy wipes tears from her face and turns her head back for one last look.

Lulu is hopping after them. They stop the car, pick her up and drop her back with the others. Again, Mandy takes one last tearful look, and again sees Lulu bounding after them. On the third failed attempt, they pitch a tent for the night. But Lulu sleeps in the car; determined to not be left behind in the morning.

Mandy brings her home and places her in the yard with older kangaroos that can't be released because they are blind or disabled. Now Lulu plays with her besties in the yard. She still races towards Mandy for cuddles and tries to jump inside her fluffy dressing gown – but now Lulu's a hefty five-year-old adult!

Red kangaroos can hop at up to 70 kilometres per hour and leap 9 metres in one bound.

KA KITE, A FEISTY FALCON

A falcon (kārearea) soars high, scouring for prey. He sees a starling darting across a paddock, so swiftly changes direction, swerving down to catch it with his talons. But as he swoops back up, a loud bang startles him. He feels severe pain in his left wing. He's been shot! The falcon lets go of the starling and plunges down onto the hard earth, falling unconscious.

The kārearea wakes up at Massey University Wildbase Hospital. Vets have inserted a pin into his hollow wing bone, hoping it will bind it together and harden. The wing aches, and the falcon is dizzy from the anaesthetic. He drifts in and out of consciousness for two weeks.

When he next wakes up, he's in a cage at the Wingspan National Bird of Prey Centre, a falcon recovery centre. Keeper Debbie Stewart holds the kārearea in her gloved hand; his wing droops low. "Poor thing, I hope you make it," she says to the rare falcon.

An Ōpōtiki family sponsors the kārearea and calls it 'Ka Kite', hoping they'll one day bid it goodbye and he'll fly off.

Every morning, Debbie weighs Ka Kite on the scales and sees he's underweight. He nips her.

With their extra-keen eyesight, falcons can scan the paddocks below as they fly, picking up the trail of an animal's urine and droppings which are only visible in ultraviolet light.

"Hey, don't bite the hand that feeds you." She laughs and offers him cut-up pheasant meat. The falcon devours it and looks for more. "All right, greedy," she says, handing him some more, "we need to build you up if you're going to fly again."

It takes three weeks for him to stop nipping Debbie. She senses the bird trusts her now. She places him a short distance away and holds food in her hand. He hops over. She carries on this routine, day by day, until he flies the distance. Then she moves him further and further away; building up his confidence.

Next, Debbie introduces a lure – a piece of leather on a string. She swings the lure round and round in a circle and lets it flump onto the ground. Ka Kite pounces on it. "Good boy," says Debbie. She's beginning to feel he might survive in the wild, after all. Soon he's catching the lure on the wing. Debbie can't wait to tell the sponsor.

The next day, Ka Kite clutches onto her gloved hand, and she saunters outside to the waiting crowd, who have gathered at Wingspan. Debbie introduces Ka Kite and then throws a piece of meat into the air. Ka Kite flies vertically upwards to catch it. Next, she encourages him to fly off, then swings the lure five times and throws it out. Ka Kite lunges for the meat attached to the end and, when he catches it, flies off to eat it. For thirty minutes, Ka Kite flies back and forth, showing the awed crowd the speed and manoeuvrability of his flying. Afterwards, he lets people hold him in their gloved hands so they can take a photo with him. He's a great ambassador for the centre.

One spring afternoon during his flight display, he tilts his head and looks skyward. A juvenile falcon flies over the centre and lands in one of the nearby gum trees. Debbie hasn't seen a wild falcon near their centre before. Nor has Ka Kite. He flies off to join the female.

Debbie doesn't see Ka Kite for a few days, and then one afternoon he flies over with his mate. He perches in his favourite eucalyptus tree and watches them. When the bird sanctuary moves to a new centre, Debbie thinks she won't see Ka Kite again. But several days later he turns up at the new site. He doesn't come close. It seems that he just wants to know they are still around if he ever needs them. Debbie is pleased he's out in the wild again – her job is done.

TAYLOR, A KOALA DETECTOR DOG

When Ryan Tate brings a 10-week old springer spaniel home, the pup is so excited she sprints round and round, and wags her tail and backside so vigorously, she nearly falls over. Jen, Ryan's wife and co-trainer, says, "Looks like we'll have some work calming Taylor down before we can train her."

But Ryan knows this energiser bunny will be perfect on detection jobs. Springer spaniels are born to retrieve – they pick up animals softly in their mouth and bring them back to their handler.

Over the next seven months, Ryan and Jen teach Taylor general obedience skills, how to respond to verbal and hand commands, as well as detection skills. She learns to associate certain smells with her favourite reward, which drives her to locate the scent wherever possible.

Ryan's two-year-old son Lennox teaches Taylor how to play fetch. The two have bonded from toddler and pup stage and spend most days playing together. Taylor even helps Lennox with chores. She collects the warm eggs in her soft mouth from the chook house and deposits them at the back door.

At 11 months old, Taylor is ready for her first job. The Macquarie Hospital team asks them to survey the area for koala. "Find koala!" Ryan instructs Taylor. Off she sprints at full speed, racing around trees, trying to pick up the scent. Very soon she stops, sits down and looks up a tree. Ryan marks it on his map and gives Taylor a treat. At the end of the job, Ryan can report back to Macquarie Hospital that it is a nationally important area, as koalas are abundant.

After that, Ryan and Taylor are employed on many jobs searching for koala, endangered quoll, and invasive pests such as mice, rats, rabbits, cats and foxes.

One day they receive an urgent callout. Taylor is needed to find koalas in the wildfires blazing around New South Wales and, later, Melbourne. When they arrive near the edge of a burn zone, the team have a safety briefing first, followed by a site check. If there are any smoking trees or naked flames within the search area, Taylor is stood down. Once it is deemed safe, Taylor searches the scorched earth for scat and sniffs the air for fur smell. Whenever she finds a koala, the emergency team catch the singed koala. Taylor and Ryan leave them to it and continue looking for more koalas.

On one job, the team park their vehicles and are doing a reconnaissance, when radio communication tells them the wind has changed and they need to leave immediately. Everyone bustles back into the cars, including the detection dogs. They race out, just in time. Soon the area is enveloped in flames.

During the 2019-20 wildfires, Taylor rescues 20 koalas. For the rest of the year they'll be surveying properties, post fires, looking for individuals that might be suffering due to lack of habitat.

In between jobs, Taylor learns how to relax back home. If she could, she would work every minute of every day. She's the most fearless and dedicated dog Ryan has ever worked with. When she's been told to stay outside, sometimes she'll turn the doorknob, push open the door with her nose, then wait. She knows she's not supposed to come inside until welcomed in. Then she slinks inside, making sure not to make eye contact, and lies down.

At home, Taylor is a troublemaker, revving up the other dogs and stealing their toys. But once in the car, she's all ready to go – a most enthusiastic detector dog.

A dog's sense of smell is many thousands of times better than a human's. With training, they can sniff out bombs, drugs, pursue a suspect, or even detect disease in a human.

SIROCCO, THE KĀKĀPŌ AMBASSADOR

Sirocco hatches late in March 1997 along with his brother Tiwai. His mother, Zephyr, keeps them warm under her soft feathers, but the howling wind and cool temperatures on Codfish Island (to the west of Stewart Island) are enough to give Sirocco a chill. Soon he is very sick with a cold. Codfish Island rangers know that if they don't interfere, Sirocco will not live much longer.

The ranger takes the young kākāpō back to the hut and hand feeds him. A year later, he is released back into the wild. But he has grown used to humans feeding him, so visits them every night. He wants some more treats, such as macadamia nuts, corn, carrots, broccoli, kumara and parrot pellets. He can't find those delicious foods in the bush. And he misses human company.

At six years old, Sirocco scrapes out a bowl in the ground, fluffs himself up and booms his mating call. Awesome, the rangers think, he's going to breed with a female kākāpō. But Sirocco only has eyes for humans! Whenever the conservationists head to the toilet during the night, Sirocco tries to get their attention. Oh dear, we need to send him further away, the rangers think. But he always finds his way back. They send him to Maud Island in the Marlborough Sounds … but he just makes friends with the ranger's children.

Kākāpō are the rarest, heaviest, and the only flightless and nocturnal parrot in the world. They have whiskers like a cat to help them walk around at night. They growl like a dog, boom like a bullfrog, and *ching!* like finger cymbals.

Sirocco has imprinted on humans and probably will never mate with another kākāpō. In fact, Sirocco has a habit of climbing up people's arms, sitting on their head and flapping his wings vigorously. One such incident is filmed and viewed on YouTube over a million times, making him an international superstar.

To curb his unusual behaviour, an American animal behaviourist trains Sirocco to transfer his attentions elsewhere. But what to use? They soon realise a toy owl won't work – it doesn't look human enough. A conservationist suggests they use his shoe, which Sirocco is fond of stealing. And it works.

Though it is a shame Sirocco won't help increase the small population of kākāpō (only 205 in 2021), he makes an excellent ambassador for the only nocturnal, non-flying parrot in the world.

Soon he is travelling all around New Zealand, and thousands visit him at their local zoo. He even spends a day in Parliament where he is officially recognised as the spokesperson for conservation. The funds raised through Sirocco's work and sponsorship enable the Kākāpō recovery team to help the critically endangered parrots more intensively. The rangers set up feeding stations to supplement kākāpō food in lean years. They monitor and manage kākāpō nests during the breeding season, which enables them to double their population. And every year they do a health check and change each adult kākāpō's transmitter.

When Sirocco's transmitter falls off, he goes missing for two years!

The Maud Island rangers search for their star bird. They arrange his favourite food in feeding stations, position cameras over them and sit back and wait. A couple of weeks later, Sirocco jumps onto one of the stations and pecks at his favourite food – macadamia nuts. The rangers race to the station, catch him, place a new transmitter on him and do a medical check. Sirocco takes it all in his stride, happy to be around humans again. The nation (and his thousands of overseas followers), breathe a sigh of relief that their kākāpō rock star is still alive.

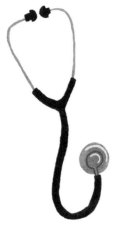

THE ROLE OF WILDLIFE CENTRES, SANCTUARIES & ZOOS

WILDLIFE CENTRES

Wildlife centres care for endangered wild animals. They might have received them from a wildlife hospital and help with their recovery. Once they are recovered, they'll release them back where they were found, if safe, or to a nearby conservation reserve. If the wildlife centre has a veterinarian, they'll treat the animal and care for it until it is old enough or healthy enough to care for itself in the wild. Most wildlife centres rely on donations to pay for the care and food for the animals.

Willowbank Wildlife Reserve Centre

SANCTUARIES

Some sanctuaries breed rare animals, others rescue animals, whether it's a farm animal, domesticated animal or wild creature. The animal might have been treated cruelly, living in inhumane conditions, or been kidnapped from a young age from its parent and been sold off at a market. Keepers at sanctuaries believe every animal has the right to kind and respectful care.

WILDLIFE HOSPITALS

If a sick or injured animal needs medical care, wildlife officers might take an animal to a wildlife hospital first. The veterinarians operate, x-ray and medicate the animal. When it is conscious and out of the danger zone, the animal is then sent to a wildlife centre to recover.

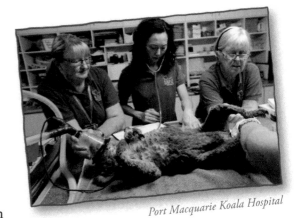

Port Macquarie Koala Hospital

During the wildfires that blazed around Australia in 2019-20, the wildlife centres and hospitals were very busy saving burnt animals, especially koalas. Birds can fly off, kangaroos can hop away, and emus can run, but the slow-moving koalas were often stuck in the middle of burning forests. Their response to fire is to climb high up into the canopy of the forest. Generally, flames flash to the next tree, rather than travel higher. But the wildfires that swept most of Australia in 2019-20 burned at high intensity. Some trees exploded and sent sparks off in every direction. It is estimated that around 8,000 koalas might have died and some species of native animals have become extinct in these wildfires.

Fires aren't the only problem for wild animals in Australia and New Zealand. Droughts leave animals desperate for water and food;

many are hit by vehicles; and predators injure or kill animals. Donations enable hospitals to finance drinking stations for wildlife in burnt and drought areas, and pay for vets and caregivers to look after injured or sick animals.

ZOOS

When zoos first began, centuries ago, their purpose was to show spectators animals from different parts of the world. And animals such as chimpanzees were sometimes used to entertain the visitors. Since then attitudes to animals have changed significantly. Zoos are now centres for conservation, education, research and recreation. They run breeding programmes for endangered species, as well as travelling to countries nearby to help them save their indigenous animals.

Some zoos have their own medical centres and treat sick and injured wildlife onsite. Zoos also educate the public about the natural world, helping to raise awareness about the problems species face and how they can be helped. Scientists at the zoo share information with other scientists around the world about what they've learnt about endangered species and conservation projects they are undertaking. Most zoos rely on ticket sales to pay for the animals' food and care so they schedule various activities to draw people to their zoos. Most of the activities will have an underlying conservation or educational message.

Auckland Zoo

ACKNOWLEDGEMENTS AND PHOTO CREDITS

Thanks to the following for giving up their time to be interviewed and/or sending photographs.

Brightside Farm Sanctuary: (Einstein) Emma Haswell, founder. Department of Conservation: (Nigel) Chris Bell, ranger; (Sirocco) Chris Burmingham; (Tumbles) Julie Harvey, takahē advocacy ranger; (Flint) Richard Johnston, conservation dog handler. Glenn Druery (Gus). Edgars Mission: (Little Miss Sunshine) Pam Ahern, Founder & Director; Kyle Behrend, Communications. Friends of Mana Island: (Nigel) Philippa Sargent, Communications; Mara Bell. Horse & Pony Magazine: (Charisma). Kangaroo Haven: (Lulu) Mandy Watson, Founder. Kea Conservation Trust: (Ken-Joe) Tamsin Orr-Walker, Laura Young. Elizabeth Macdonald: (Flint). Magnetic Island Koala Hospital: (Crikey & Pumpkin) Dr Ali Bee, veterinarian; Sophie Bee, koala whisperer. National Aquarium of New Zealand: (Inky) Rachel Haydon, General Manager. New Zealand Herald/Alan Gibson (Moko). Pacific Whale Foundation: (Migaloo). Pelican Lagoon Research & Wildlife Centre: (Big Mama) Dr Peggy Rismiller, Scientist; Mike McKelvey, Biologist. Penguin Foundation: (Little Blue penguins) Jaquelina Ferreira, Administration Officer. Pūkaha National Wildlife Centre: (Kahurangi) Tara Swan, Communications Advisor & Captive Breeding Keeper. Queensland Parks & Wildlife Service/David Fleay Wildlife Park: (Wally) Emily Wanray, ranger. Royal Albatross Centre: (Rob) Laura and Sophie Barker. SEA LIFE Kelly Tarlton's Aquarium: (Calvin) Madeline Seaman, aquarist; Toby Butland, Marketing Manager. Southland Museum & Art Gallery: (Henry) Lindsay Hazley, Curator. State Library Victoria: (Phar Lap) Charles D. Pratt. Tate Animals: (Taylor) Ryan & Jen Tate, animal trainers. Te Anau Bird Sanctuary: (Tumbles) Catherine Brimecombe, keeper; Anja Kohler of Capture It Photography. The Oceania Project: (Migaloo) Wally Franklin. The Wildlife Hospital Trust: (Chrystall) Jordana Whyte, Manager; Fergus Sutherland. Twitter First Cat of NZ: (Paddles). Willowbank Wildlife Reserve: (Royal) Kirsty Willis, General Manager; Averill Moser-Rust, Bethany Brett. Wingspan Birds of Prey Trust: (Ka Kite) Debbie Stewart MNZM, Founder & Director, Kurien Yohannan. Wombat Awareness Organisation: (Barney & Pebbles) Brigitte Stevens, Founder.

FURTHER INVESTIGATION

Check out the wonderful wildlife centres, sanctuaries and hospitals mentioned in the book to find out more about the glorious work they are doing to save animals. Many of these centres operate on donations only. If you would like to help them, look for a sponsorship page on their website.

Brightside Farm Sanctuary: www.brightside.org.au
NZ Department of Conservation programmes: www.doc.govt.nz (search: kākāpō recovery, takahē recovery, Te Anau bird sanctuary, kea)
Tate Animals Detection dogs: www.tateanimals.com
Edgar Mission Farm Sanctuary: www.edgarsmission.org.au
Kangaroo Haven Wildlife Rescue: www.kangaroohavenwildliferescue.com.au
Sea Life, Kelly Tarlton's: www.kellytarltons.co.nz
Magnetic Island Koala Hospital: www.magneticislandkoalahospital.com.au
Mana Island Trust: www.manaisland.org.nz/current-projects
Napier Aquarium: www.nationalaquarium.co.nz
Oceania Project whale research: www.oceania.org.au
Pelican Lagoon Research and Wildlife Centre: www.echidna.edu.au
Penguin Place: www.penguinplace.co.nz
Phillip Island Penguin Parade: www.penguins.org.au/attractions/penguin-parade
Platypus: www.fleayswildlife.com.au
Port Macquarie Wildlife Hospital: www.koalahospital.org.au
Pūkaha National Wildlife Centre: www.pukaha.org.nz
Royal Albatross Centre: www.albatross.org.nz
Society of the Prevention of Cruelty to Animals: www.spca.nz
Tuatarium: www.southlandmuseum.co.nz
Wildlife Hospital, Dunedin: www.wildlifehospitaldunedin.org.nz
Willowbank Wildlife Reserve: www.willowbank.co.nz
Wingspan National Bird of Prey Centre: www.wingspan.co.nz
Wombat Sanctuary: www.wombatawareness.com

BIBLIOGRAPHY

Ballance, A. (Mar, 2018) 'Turnaround in takahē's fortunes' from *Our Changing World*, Radio New Zealand.
Bekoff, M. (Oct 2000) 'Animal Emotions: Exploring Passionate Natures' in *BioScience*, Vol 50, Issue 10, Pages 861-870.
Connor, S. (Sept, 2011) 'Study proves that animals have different personalities', retrieved from: https://www.independent.co.uk/environment/nature/study-proves-animals-have-different-personalities
Ell, S. (2012) *Sirocco: The Rock-star Kakapo*, Random House, Auckland.
Graham-McLay, C. (31 Oct 2019) 'Amused us for years: Rob the unappealing albatross finally finds a mate', from www.theguardian.com
Montgomery, S. (2010) *Kakapo Rescue: Saving the World's Strangest Parrot*, Houghton Mifflin, USA.
National Geographic, 'Platypus', from www.nationalgeographic.com/animals/mammals
Putt, G. & McCord, P. (2009) *Phar Lap: The Untold Story*, BAS Publishing, Australia.
Shivak, J.A. (1 Dec 2017) 'Do animals have personalities? Why scientists are starting to admit they do', from www.nbcnews.com
Singhal, P. (Dec, 2019) 'Most popular cat in the country: Gus enters dog race, comes first in category' from *The Sydney Morning Herald*.
Todd, M. (1989) *Charisma*, Raupo Publishing, Auckland.